CONTINENTS IN CLOSE-U

EUROPE

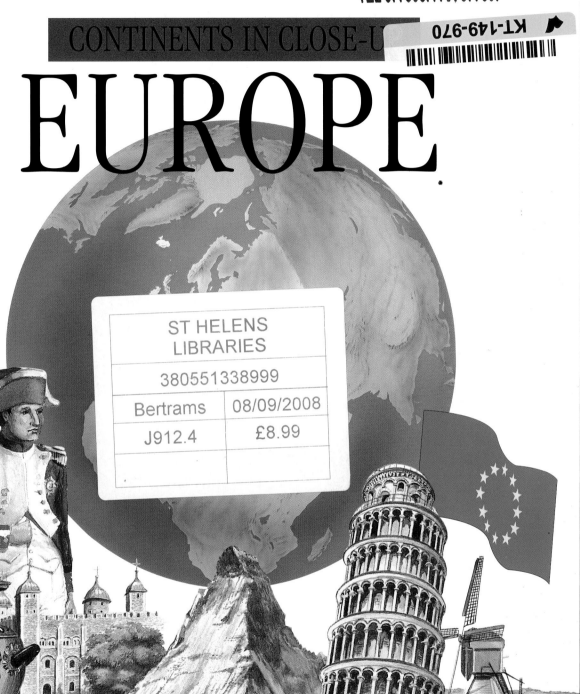

MALCOLM PORTER and KEITH LYE

A Cherrytree Book

Designed and produced by
AS Publishing
Text by Keith Lye
Illustrated by Malcolm Porter and Raymond Turvey

New edition published 2008 by
Cherrytree Books, part of the
Evans Publishing Group
2a Portman Mansions
Chiltern Street
London W1U 6NR

Copyright © Malcolm Porter and AS Publishing

British Library Cataloguing in Publication data

Porter, Malcolm
  Europe. - (Continents in close-up)
  1.Children's atlases
  2.Europe - Maps for children
  I.Title II.Lye, Keith
  912.4

ISBN 978 1842344576

Printed in Spain by Grafo SA

CONTINENTS IN CLOSE-UP

EUROPE

This illustrated atlas combines maps, pictures, flags, globes,
information panels, diagrams and charts to give an overview of
the whole continent, a closer look at each of its countries and
at the Atlantic and Arctic oceans.

COUNTRY CLOSE-UPS

Each double-page spread has these
features:

Introduction The author introduces the
most important facts about the country
or region.

Globes A globe on which you can see the
country's or region's position in the
continent and the world.

Flags Every country's flag is shown.

Information panels Every country has an
information panel which gives its area,
population and capital, and where
possible its currency, religions, languages,
main towns and government.

Pictures Important features of each
country are illustrated and captioned to
give a flavour of the country. You can
find out about physical features, famous
people, ordinary people, animals, plants,
places, products and much more.

Maps Every country is shown on a
clear, accurate map. To get the most from
the maps it helps to know the symbols
which are shown in the key on the
opposite page.

Land You can see by the colouring on
the map where the land is forested,
frozen or desert.

Height Relief hill shading shows where
the mountain ranges are. Individual
mountains are marked by a triangle.

Direction Except for the map of the
Arctic, all of the maps are drawn
with north at the top of the page.

Scale All of the maps are drawn to scale
so that you can find the distance
between places in miles or kilometres.

```
0                                    200 miles
├──────────────┬──────────────┤
0                      200 kilometres
```

KEY TO MAPS

FRANCE	Country name
Lapland	Region
~~	Country border
■	More than 1 million people*
•	More than 500,000 people
·	Less than 500,000 people
□	Country capital
ᴬᴸᴾˢ	Mountain range
▲ Mont Blanc 4807m	Mountain with its height
∴ Stonehenge	Archaeological site

Rhine	River
⟶	Canal
⬭	Lake
─┼─	Dam
⬭	Island

	Forest
	Crops
	Dry grassland
	Desert
	Tundra
	Polar

Population figures in all cases are estimates, based on the most recent censuses where available or a variety of other sources.

CONTINENT CLOSE-UPS

People and Beliefs Map of population densities; chart of percentage of population by country; chart of areas of countries; map of religions.

Climate and Vegetation Map of vegetation from polar to desert; maps of winter and summer temperatures; map of annual rainfall.

Ecology and Environment Map of environmental damage to land and sea; maps showing deaths caused by heart disease, cancers and fatal road accidents; panel on endangered animals and plants.

Economy Map of agricultural and industrial products; chart of gross domestic product for individual countries; panel on per capita gross domestic products; map of sources of energy.

Politics and History Panel of great events; map of location of major events in European history; timeline of important dates; maps of prehistoric sites, the Roman empire, 20th century conflicts and the European Community.

Oceans Maps of the Atlantic and Arctic oceans, and panels of statistics.

Index All the names on the maps and in the picture captions can be found in the index at the end of the book.

CONTENTS

Reindeer
see page 7

EUROPE

Europe is the sixth largest continent, covering about seven per cent of the world's land area. Only Australia is smaller. Europe was the home of several major civilizations and its culture has had a great influence on the rest of the world.

In the east, Europe borders Asia. The boundary with Asia runs along the Ural Mountains and the Ural River to the Caspian Sea and then through the Caucasus Mountains. About a quarter of Russia lies in Europe, while the rest is in Asia. Smaller parts of four other countries also lie in Europe.

European Union This is an alliance of 27 European countries that work together to create a single economy and, through friendly co-operation, promote democracy and prevent wars. The headquarters is in Brussels (above), the parliament in Strasbourg.

Napoleon I (1769-1821) was a great military leader who became emperor of France. His armies conquered an empire that covered most of central and western Europe. Europe has been the scene of many great wars.

EUROPE
Area: 10,443,000sq km (4,032,000sq miles)
Population: 700,000,000
Number of independent countries: 44
(including European Russia, but not Azerbaijan, Georgia, Kazakhstan and Turkey, which are mainly in Asia)

ICELAND

ATLANTIC OCEAN

NORWAY

SWEDEN

North Sea

IRELAND

UNITED KINGDOM

DENMARK

Baltic Se

NETHERLANDS

BELGIUM

GERMANY

POLAN

LUXEMBOURG

CZECH REP.

Bay of Biscay

FRANCE

LIECHTENSTEIN

SLOVA

SWITZERLAND

AUSTRIA

HUNGA

SLOVENIA

CROATIA

ANDORRA

MONACO

SAN MARINO

BOSNIA& HERZEGOVI

PORTUGAL

SPAIN

ITALY

MONTENE

VATICAN CITY

GIBRALTAR (UK)

MEDITERRANEAN SEA

MALTA

| 0 | 250 miles |
| 0 | 250 kilometres |

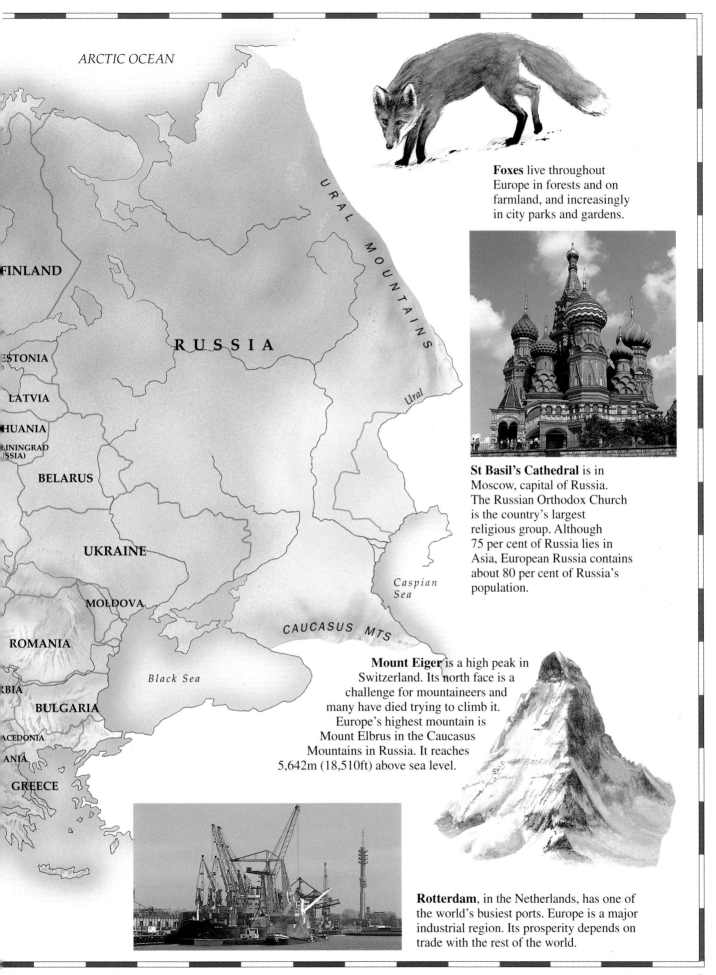

ARCTIC OCEAN

URAL MOUNTAINS

FINLAND

ESTONIA

LATVIA

HUANIA

LININGRAD
USSIA)

BELARUS

UKRAINE

MOLDOVA

ROMANIA

RBIA

BULGARIA

ACEDONIA

ANIA

GREECE

RUSSIA

Ural

Caspian
Sea

CAUCASUS MTS

Black Sea

Foxes live throughout
Europe in forests and on
farmland, and increasingly
in city parks and gardens.

St Basil's Cathedral is in
Moscow, capital of Russia.
The Russian Orthodox Church
is the country's largest
religious group. Although
75 per cent of Russia lies in
Asia, European Russia contains
about 80 per cent of Russia's
population.

Mount Eiger is a high peak in
Switzerland. Its north face is a
challenge for mountaineers and
many have died trying to climb it.
Europe's highest mountain is
Mount Elbrus in the Caucasus
Mountains in Russia. It reaches
5,642m (18,510ft) above sea level.

Rotterdam, in the Netherlands, has one of
the world's busiest ports. Europe is a major
industrial region. Its prosperity depends on
trade with the rest of the world.

NORTHERN EUROPE

Northern Europe contains Scandinavia, a region that consists of Norway and Sweden. It also includes Finland and the small country of Denmark.

   The climate is mostly unsuitable for farming, except in the south. The region's resources include Norway's oil, which it gets from the North Sea, its many rivers, which are used to produce hydroelectricity, and huge forests. Manufacturing is now the most valuable activity in all four countries.

DENMARK

Area: 43,094sq km (16,639sq miles)
Highest point: 173m (568ft)
Population: 5,451,000
Capital and largest city: Copenhagen (pop 1,066,000)
Other large cities: Århus (229,000) Odense (146,000) Ålborg (122,000)
Official language: Danish
Religion: Christianity (Lutheran 95%)
Government: Monarchy
Currency: Danish krone

FINLAND

Area: 338,145sq km (130,559sq miles)
Highest point: Mount Haltia 1,324m (4,344ft)
Population: 5,231,000
Capital and largest city: Helsinki (pop 1,075,000)
Other large cities: Espoo (224,000), Tampere (201,000), Vantaa (184,000), Turku (175,000), Oulu (126,000)
Official languages: Finnish, Swedish
Religion: Christianity (Lutheran 84%)
Government: Republic
Currency: Euro

NORWAY

Area: 323,877sq km (125,050sq miles)
Highest point: Galdhøppigen 2,469m (8,100ft)
Population: 4,612,000
Capital and largest city: Oslo (pop 795,000)
Other large cities: Bergen (211,000) Stavanger (169,000) Trondheim (144,000)
Official language: Norwegian
Religion: Christianity (Lutheran 85%)
Government: Monarchy
Currency: Norwegian krone

Fiords are long, narrow inlets of sea that stretch along the ragged, mountainous coast of Norway. One of them, called Sogne Fiord, extends 200km (124 miles) inland.

Oil is extracted from deposits under the North Sea. Fuels and fuel products are Norway's leading exports. Farming, forestry, fishing and manufacturing are other major activities in northern Europe.

SWEDEN

Area: 449,964sq km (173,732sq miles)
Highest point: Mount Kebnekaise 2,111m (6,926ft)
Population: 9,017,000
Capital and largest city: Stockholm (pop 1,697,000)
Other large cities: Göteborg (481,000) Malmö (269,000)
Official language: Swedish
Religion: Christianity (Church of Sweden 87%)
Government: Monarchy
Currency: Swedish krona

ATLANTIC OCEAN

Trondheim

Ålesund

▲ *Galdhøppigen 2469m*

Bergen

NORWAY

Glåma

Stavanger

Oslo

Skien

Fredrikstad

Lake Vänern

Kristiansand

Lak Vätter

Skagerrak

Borås

Göteborg

North Sea

Ålborg

Kattegat

Vä

Jutland

Århus

173m

DENMARK

Esbjerg

Copenhagen

Odense

Malmö

Bornholt

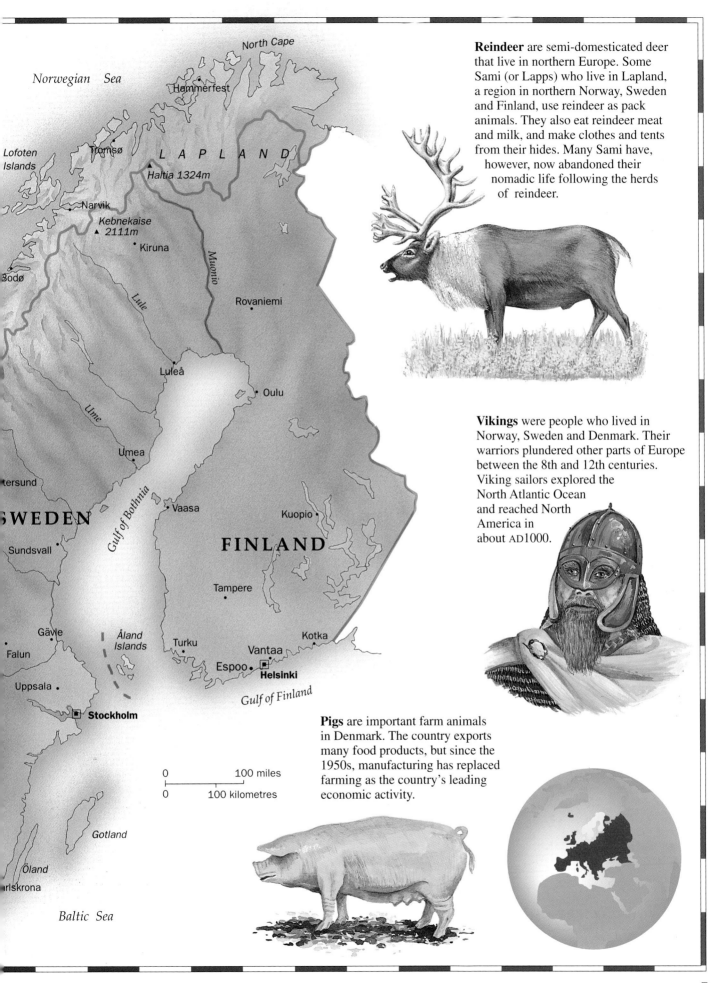

Reindeer are semi-domesticated deer that live in northern Europe. Some Sami (or Lapps) who live in Lapland, a region in northern Norway, Sweden and Finland, use reindeer as pack animals. They also eat reindeer meat and milk, and make clothes and tents from their hides. Many Sami have, however, now abandoned their nomadic life following the herds of reindeer.

Vikings were people who lived in Norway, Sweden and Denmark. Their warriors plundered other parts of Europe between the 8th and 12th centuries. Viking sailors explored the North Atlantic Ocean and reached North America in about AD1000.

Pigs are important farm animals in Denmark. The country exports many food products, but since the 1950s, manufacturing has replaced farming as the country's leading economic activity.

Norwegian Sea

North Cape

Hammerfest

Lofoten Islands

L A P L A N D

Tromsø

▲ Haltia 1324m

Narvik

Kebnekaise
▲ 2111m

Kiruna

Bodø

Lule

Muonio

Rovaniemi

Ume

Luleå

Oulu

Umeå

tersund

Gulf of Bothnia

Vaasa

Kuopio

FINLAND

SWEDEN

Sundsvall

Tampere

Gävle

Åland Islands

Turku

Kotka

Falun

Vantaa

Espoo

Uppsala

Helsinki

Stockholm

Gulf of Finland

0   100 miles

0   100 kilometres

Gotland

Öland

rlskrona

Baltic Sea

ICELAND

Iceland, in the North Atlantic Ocean, is often called the 'land of ice and fire'. Large bodies of ice cover about one-eighth of the land and the country has about 200 volcanoes. The main industry is fishing and fish processing.

 ICELAND

Area: 103,000sq km (39,769sq miles)
Highest point: Hvannadalshnúkur 2,119m (6,952ft)
Population: 299,000
Capital: Reykjavik (pop 184,000)
Official language: Icelandic
Religion: Christianity (Lutheran 85%)
Government: Republic
Currency: Icelandic krona

Geysers are hot springs that throw up high jets of steam and hot water. The water is heated by underground volcanic rocks. It is used to heat buildings and supply homes with hot tap water.

Fishing is important in the waters around Iceland. Fish and fish products account for more than half of the country's exports. Iceland has little farmland, though some farmers keep sheep and cattle.

Ísafjördhur

Siglufjördhur

Blönduos

Akureyri

Seydisfjördhur

ICELAND

Vatnajökull

Hofn

Keflavik ▣ Reykjavik

Hafnarfjördhur

▲ *Hvannadalshnúkur 2119m*

ATLANTIC OCEAN

Heimaey

Vik

Surtsey

0		50 miles
0		50 kilometres

Surtsey is a volcanic island that appeared off southern Iceland in 1963. It was named after Surt, the Norse god of fire.

IRELAND

Ireland consists of the Republic of Ireland, which makes up five-sixths of the island, and Northern Ireland which is part of the United Kingdom (see page 10). Farming is important in Ireland, but manufacturing and new technology and service industries are the most valuable activities.

 IRELAND

Area: 70,284sq km (27,137sq miles)
Highest point: Carrauntoohill 1,041m (3,141ft)
Population: 4,062,000
Capital and largest city: Dublin (pop 1,015,000)
Other large cities: Cork (186,000)
Official languages: Irish, English
Religion: Christianity (Roman Catholic 88%)
Government: Republic
Currency: Euro

Giant's Causeway is probably Northern Ireland's best-known tourist attraction. It was formed when molten lava cooled to form masses of six-sided columns made of a rock called basalt.

Shamrock is Ireland's national symbol. It is a kind of clover that, according to legend, St Patrick planted. Its three leaves represent the Holy Trinity.

Celtic crosses and other carved stone monuments are found throughout Ireland.

Potatoes, barley, sugar beet and wheat are leading crops in Ireland. Cattle and dairy produce are important, as are pigs and sheep.

UNITED KINGDOM

The United Kingdom of Great Britain and Northern Ireland (often called the UK, or Britain) includes England, Scotland and Wales, which are together called Great Britain, and Northern Ireland (see map on page 9).

The Industrial Revolution began in England in the late 18th century and today the country plays a major part in world trade. It contains some of the most densely populated areas in Europe.

UNITED KINGDOM

Area: 243,305sq km (93,941sq miles)
Highest point: Ben Nevis 1,343m (4,406ft)
Population: 60,609,000
Capital and largest city: London (pop 7,619,000)
Other large cities: Birmingham (2,243,000)
Manchester (2,223,000)
Leeds (1,417,000)
Official language: English
Religion: Christianity (71%)
Government: Monarchy
Currency: Pound sterling

ENGLAND
Area: 130,395sq km (50,346sq miles)
Population: 50,911,000
Capital: London (pop 7,619,000)

NORTHERN IRELAND
Area: 13,843sq km (5,345sq miles)
Population: 1,703,000
Capital: Belfast (pop 277,000)

SCOTLAND
Area: 78,313sq km (30,237sq miles)
Population: 5,057,000
Capital: Edinburgh (pop 449,000)

WALES
Area: 20,754sq km (8,013sq miles)
Population: 2,938,000
Capital: Cardiff (pop 305,000)

ISLE OF MAN & CHANNEL ISLANDS
The Isle of Man in the Irish Sea and the Channel Islands off the coast of northwest France are British dependencies, but they are not part of the United Kingdom.

William Shakespeare (1564-1616) is widely regarded as the world's greatest poet and dramatist. Britain has also produced many other celebrated writers, and the language in which they have written is now spoken in many countries.

Stonehenge is an ancient monument in southern England. It is a circle of huge stones that were probably used for religious purposes. It was built between about 2800 and 1500 BC.

Sheep are raised in highland areas, cattle and pigs on lowland farms. Agriculture is important but the country imports food. Most of its wealth comes from manufacturing, trade and services such as banking, insurance, finance and tourism.

John o' Groats
Wick
Lewis
North West Highlands
Hebrides
Inverness
Skye
Loch Ness
Spey
Grampian Mts
Fort William
Ben Nevis 1343m
Dunde
Perth
Loch Lomond
SCOTLAND
Glasgow
Clyde
Edinbur
Ayr
Dumfries
Carlis
Isle of Man
Scafell Pr 978m
Douglas
Blackpool
Liverpool
Bangor
Snowdon 1085m
IRISH SEA
WALES
Aberystwyth
Swansea
New
Cardiff
Brist
Exeter
Plymouth
Penzance
Land's End
Isles of Scilly

Orkney Islands

•Wick

Shetland Islands

•Lerwick

•rdeen

Golf developed in Scotland, where the first organized golf club was set up in 1744. Soccer is, however, by far the most popular sport in the United Kingdom.

NORTH SEA

•rwick-upon-Tweed

•Newcastle upon Tyne
•Sunderland

•Middlesbrough

•York
•Bradford
■ **Leeds**
•nchester

•Kingston upon Hull

• Sheffield

•e-on-Trent
•erby •Nottingham

ENGLAND

•Leicester
•olverhampton
•Coventry
mingham

•Norwich

Cambridge

Northampton

• Ipswich

Oxford   • Luton

Thames ■
London

Reading

Stonehenge

Dover

Southampton Brighton
• Portsmouth
•urnemouth

Isle of Wight

English Channel

London Eye Built by the River Thames to mark the millennium, this observation wheel is 135m (443ft) high. From the top you can see for 40km (25 miles).

Puffins are sea birds found mostly on the north and west coasts of Britain. The country has many animal species, though numbers have declined because of human population pressures and pollution.

Channel Islands

Guernsey

FRANCE

Jersey

London was founded by the Romans in AD 43 on the River Thames. It has many historic buildings. The business heart of London, called the City of London, is an internationally important financial centre.

0	50 miles
0	50 kilometres

LOW COUNTRIES

The Low Countries lie at the western end of a huge plain that extends across Europe from the North Sea to the Ural Mountains in Russia. Much of the land is flat. Large areas, especially in the Netherlands, were once under the sea. They would still be flooded if the Dutch had not built dikes (strong sea walls). Farming is important in this region, but manufacturing is the most valuable activity.

BELGIUM

Area: 30,519sq km (11,783sq miles)
Highest point: Botrange Mountain 694m (2,277ft)
Population: 10,379,000
Capital and largest city: Brussels (pop 1,000,000)
Other large cities: Antwerp (455,000) Ghent (229,000)
Official languages: Dutch, French, German
Religion: Christianity (Roman Catholic 75%)
Government: Federal monarchy
Currency: Euro

LUXEMBOURG

Area: 2,586sq km (998sq miles)
Highest point: Buurgplatz 559m (1,835ft)
Population: 474,000
Capital: Luxembourg (pop 77,000)
Languages: Luxemburgian, French, German
Religion: Christianity (Roman Catholic 87%)
Government: Monarchy (Grand Duchy)
Currency: Euro

NETHERLANDS

Area: 40,844sq km (15,770sq miles)
Highest point: 321m (1,053ft)
Population: 16,491,000
Capital and largest city: Amsterdam (pop 736,000)
Other large cities: Rotterdam (599,000) The Hague (458,000)
Official language: Dutch
Religion: Christianity (Roman Catholic 31%, Dutch Reform Church 13%, Calvinist 7%)
Government: Monarchy
Currency: Euro

Windmills have been used for centuries to operate pumps to drain water from flat land in the Low Countries. Farming is a major activity. Flowers and bulbs are well-known products of the Netherlands.

Brussels has a fine city centre and is an international meeting place. It is in a bilingual (two-language) region of Belgium, where both Dutch and French are spoken. Other regions include the Dutch-speaking Flemish Region in the north and the French-speaking Walloon Region in the south.

NETHERLANDS

Frisian Islands

Leeuwarden

Groningen

Barrier Dam

IJsselmeer

Zwolle

IJssel

Apeldoorn

Almelo

Enschede

Utrecht

Rhine

Arnhem

Nijmegen

-Hertogenbosch

Maas

burg

• Eindhoven

Genk

Heerlen

Maastricht *321m*

• Liège

Botrange ▲
694m

d e n n e s

▲
Buurgplatz 559m

LUXEMBOURG

Luxembourg
◉

Esch-sur-Alzette

Barges are used to
transport goods along rivers
and canals. Rotterdam in the Netherlands
and Antwerp in Belgium are among
the world's busiest ports.

Computers and electronic products are
important in the Netherlands. The country
also produces many other technically
advanced goods. Belgium is famous for
its ancient textile industry, while
Luxembourg is a major steel producer.

Bicycles and motorcycles are
popular means of transport
across the flat countryside.
The Low Countries have a
good network of paved roads
and most families own a car.

Grand Ducal Palace This is the
home of the Grand Duke (or Duchess)
of Luxembourg, the country's head
of state. Though the countries are all
democracies, the Low Countries have
a long monarchist tradition.

GERMANY

In 1945, at the end of World War II, Germany was in ruins. From 1949, it was divided into two parts. West Germany, with aid from western countries including the United States, recovered quickly from the war. It soon became a prosperous industrial democracy. East Germany, under a Communist government, was much less prosperous. The two Germanies were reunited in 1990. This was the first of several major changes to the map of Europe that occurred during the 1990s.

GERMANY

Area: 356,980sq km (137,831sq miles)
Highest point: Zugspitze, near the Austrian border, 2,963m (9,721ft)
Population: 82,422,000
Capital and largest city: Berlin (pop 3,388,000)
Other large cities: Hamburg (1,743,000)
Munich (1,248,000)
Cologne (966,000)
Frankfurt-am-Main (644,000)
Essen (590,000)
Official language: German
Religions: Christianity (Lutheran 34%, Roman Catholic 34%), Islam 4%
Government: Federal republic
Currency: Euro

Storks can often be seen perching on nests on chimney pots. Birds and other wildlife in Germany have suffered from pollution, including acid rain, which has damaged the country's forests.

Printing The invention of movable type in the mid-15th century by the German Johannes Gutenberg speeded up book production and enabled education to spread. The Gutenberg Bible was the first Bible produced by movable type.

Brandenburg Gate This monument, built in 1791, became a symbol of a divided Europe. It stood close to the wall that the communist East German government built to prevent unauthorized crossings to the West. When the wall came down in 1989, Germans gathered at the gate to celebrate.

NORTH SEA

Flensb
Bremerhaven
Hambu
Oldenburg
Bremen
Hanov
Osnabrück
Münster
Bielefeld
Weser
Dortmund
Duisburg
Essen
Düsseldorf
Wuppertal
Kasse
Mönchengladbach
Cologne
Aachen
Bonn
G E R M
Rhine
Eifel
Koblenz
Frankfurt-am-Main
Mosel
Wiesbaden
Mainz
Darmstadt
Mannheim
Saarbrücken
Karlsruhe
Stuttgar
Baden-Baden
Black Forest
Ulr
Freiburg
Ravensbur
Lake Constance

BALTIC SEA

Kiel

Stralsund

Rostock

beck

Schwerin

Braunschweig

Harz Mts

Berlin

Potsdam

Magdeburg

Elbe

Halle

Leipzig

Meissen

Erfurt

Dresden

Chemnitz

ANY

Zwickau

Ore Mts

Main

Bayreuth

Bohemian Forest

Nuremberg

Regensburg

Danube

Passau

Augsburg

Munich

Zugspitze 2963m

Frankfurt-am-Main is a great centre of commerce and business. The city's trade fairs attract people from all over the world. It was the birthplace of Germany's greatest poet, Johann Wolfgang von Goethe.

Goethe is most famous for his verse play *Faust*. As well as great literature, Germany produced Johann Sebastian Bach, Ludwig van Beethoven, Richard Wagner and many other great composers.

Rhine This great river is a major trade route. It rises in Switzerland and flows through southwestern Germany before turning into the Netherlands and emptying into the North Sea.

German cars are known throughout the world. Germany ranks third in car production after Japan and the United States, and is one of the world's top trading nations.

0   50 miles

0   50 kilometres

MIDDLE EUROPE

Middle Europe consists of Switzerland, Austria and the tiny principality of Liechtenstein, which is sandwiched between them. Western Europe's highest mountain range, the Alps, runs through the region. The magnificent scenery and winter sports draw many tourists to the area. Manufacturing is important and the countries are prosperous. Switzerland is famous for its banks, which have investors from all over the world.

AUSTRIA

Area: 83,859sq km (32,378sq miles)
Highest point: Gross Glockner 3,797m (12,547ft)
Population: 8,193,000
Capital and largest city: Vienna (pop 2,179,000)
Other large cities: Graz (226,000)
Official language: German
Religion: Christianity (Roman Catholic 74%)
Government: Federal republic
Currency: Euro

SWITZERLAND

Area: 41,284sq km (15,940sq miles)
Highest point: Dufourspitze of Monte Rosa 4,634m (15,203ft)
Population: 7,524,000
Capital: Bern (pop 129,000)
Largest cities: Zurich (939,000)
Geneva (399,000)
Basel (176,000)
Official languages: French, German, Italian
Religion: Christianity (Roman Catholic 46%, Protestant 40%)
Government: Federal republic
Currency: Swiss franc

LIECHTENSTEIN

Area: 160sq km (62sq miles)
Population: 34,000
Capital: Vaduz (pop 5,000)
Official language: German
Religion: Christianity (Roman Catholic 76%)
Government: Monarchy (principality)
Currency: Swiss franc

Watches and precision instruments are famous Swiss products. Switzerland lacks natural resources. Its skilled workers use imported materials to make valuable products.

Alps This magnificent, snow-capped range extends from France, through Switzerland, Austria and northern Italy, into Slovenia. The most famous high peak in the Swiss Alps is the Matterhorn.

Postage stamps provide a useful source of income for Liechtenstein. Many stamps prized by collectors show paintings that belong to the country's prince.

Lake Constance
Rhine
Basel
Winterthur
Konstanz
Dornbirn
Aarau
Zurich
Sankt Gallen
Zurichsee
Vaduz
St Anto
LIECHTENSTEIN
Lucerne
Neuchâtel
Bern
Chur
Rhine
Lake Neuchâtel
SWITZERLAND
A
St Moritz
Lausanne
Lake Geneva
Geneva
Rhône
Locarno
Lugano
Matterhorn 4478m
Zermatt
Lake Maggiore
Monte Rosa 4634m

0   100 miles
0   100 kilometres

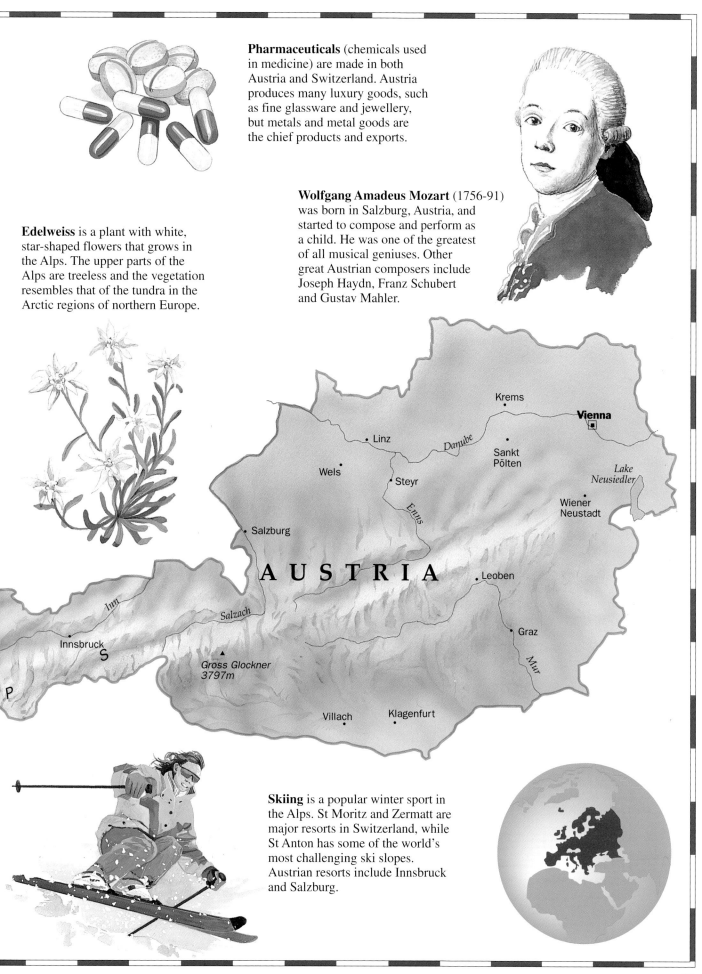

Pharmaceuticals (chemicals used in medicine) are made in both Austria and Switzerland. Austria produces many luxury goods, such as fine glassware and jewellery, but metals and metal goods are the chief products and exports.

Wolfgang Amadeus Mozart (1756-91) was born in Salzburg, Austria, and started to compose and perform as a child. He was one of the greatest of all musical geniuses. Other great Austrian composers include Joseph Haydn, Franz Schubert and Gustav Mahler.

Edelweiss is a plant with white, star-shaped flowers that grows in the Alps. The upper parts of the Alps are treeless and the vegetation resembles that of the tundra in the Arctic regions of northern Europe.

Krems
Vienna
Linz
Danube
Sankt Pölten
Wels
Lake Neusiedler
Steyr
Wiener Neustadt
Enns
Salzburg

AUSTRIA

Leoben

Inn
Salzach
Graz
Innsbruck
S
Mur
Gross Glockner
3797m

P

Villach
Klagenfurt

Skiing is a popular winter sport in the Alps. St Moritz and Zermatt are major resorts in Switzerland, while St Anton has some of the world's most challenging ski slopes. Austrian resorts include Innsbruck and Salzburg.

FRANCE

France is the largest country in western Europe. It has a beautiful landscape and fine cities with many historic buildings. It is also one of the world's top manufacturing nations and Paris is a world centre of the fashion industry. Agriculture employs only three per cent of the population, but France is western Europe's leading producer of farm products. France is famous for its excellent food and wines, and is one of the most prosperous countries in Europe.

Charles de Gaulle (1890-1970) led the French resistance to Germany in World War II. As France's president (1958-69), he tackled the problems arising from the granting of independence to France's overseas empire.

FRANCE

Area: 551,500sq km (212,935sq miles)
Highest point: Mont Blanc 4,807m (15,771ft)
Population: 60,876,000
Capital and largest city: Paris (pop 9,794,000)
Other large cities: Lyon (1,362,000)
Marseille (1,357,000)
Lille (1,007,000)
Nice (889,000)
Toulouse (761,000)
Bordeaux (754,000)
Nantes (545,000)
Strasbourg (427,000)
Official language: French
Religions: Christianity (Roman Catholic 85%), Islam 7%
Government: Republic
Currency: Euro

MONACO

Area: 1.5sq km (0.6sq miles)
Population: 33,000
Capital: Monaco (1,100)
Official language: French
Religion: Christianity (Roman Catholic 90%)
Government: Monarchy under French protection
Currency: Euro

Eiffel Tower This wrought-iron tower in Paris is the city's most famous landmark. It was built for the World Fair of 1889. Paris is a great centre of the arts and education, and also a major industrial city.

ATLANTIC OCEAN

English Channel

Cal.

Cherbourg

Le Havre

Rouer

Caen

Brest

Brittany

Rennes

Le Mans

Orléa

Nantes

Tours

Poitiers

Limog

Bay of Biscay

Bordeaux

Dordog

Garonne

Toulouse

Bayonne

P Y R E N E E

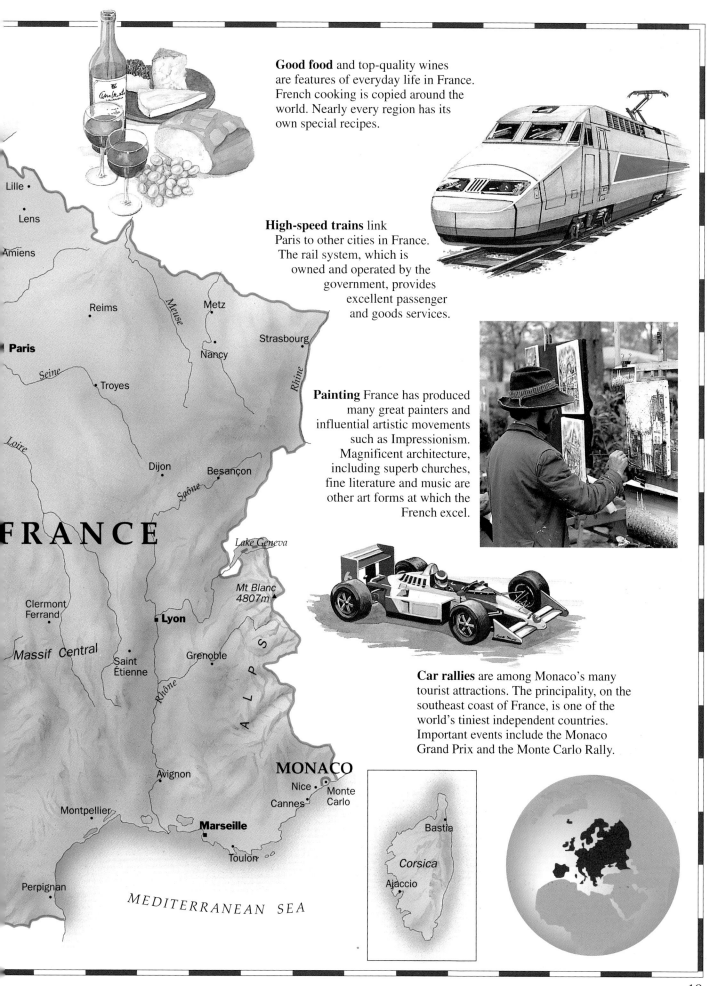

Good food and top-quality wines are features of everyday life in France. French cooking is copied around the world. Nearly every region has its own special recipes.

High-speed trains link Paris to other cities in France. The rail system, which is owned and operated by the government, provides excellent passenger and goods services.

Painting France has produced many great painters and influential artistic movements such as Impressionism. Magnificent architecture, including superb churches, fine literature and music are other art forms at which the French excel.

Car rallies are among Monaco's many tourist attractions. The principality, on the southeast coast of France, is one of the world's tiniest independent countries. Important events include the Monaco Grand Prix and the Monte Carlo Rally.

Lille •
Lens •
Amiens •
Reims •
Metz •
Strasbourg •
Paris
Nancy •
Seine
Meuse
Troyes •
Rhine
Loire
Dijon •
Besançon •
Saône
FRANCE
Lake Geneva
Mt Blanc 4807m ▲
Clermont Ferrand •
Lyon ■
A L P S
Massif Central
Grenoble •
Saint Étienne •
Rhône
Avignon •
MONACO
Nice •
Monte Carlo •
Cannes •
Montpellier •
Marseille ■
Toulon •
Perpignan •
MEDITERRANEAN SEA
Bastia •
Corsica
Ajaccio •

IBERIAN PENINSULA

The Iberian Peninsula consists of two large countries, Spain and Portugal, together with the tiny state of Andorra, in the Pyrenees Mountains in the northeast, and Gibraltar, a small British territory, in the far south. The Canary Islands off the coast of Africa also belong to Spain.

Spain is western Europe's second largest country after France. Spain's economy was shattered by a civil war (1936-39), but since the 1950s it has developed into a fairly prosperous nation. Portugal was a dictatorship from 1933 until 1968. Since 1968, its economy has grown, but it remains one of the poorer members of the European Union.

SPAIN

Area: 505,992sq km (195,365sq miles)
Highest point: Pico de Teide, in the Canary Islands, 3,718m (12,198ft)
Population: 40,000,000
Capital and largest city: Madrid (pop 5,103,000)
Other large cities: Barcelona (4,378,000) Valencia (754,000)
Languages: Castilian Spanish (official), Catalan, Galician, Basque
Religion: Christianity (Roman Catholic 94%)
Government: Monarchy
Currency: Euro

PORTUGAL

Area: 91,982sq km (35,514sq miles)
Highest point: Estrela,1,993m (6,539ft)
Population: 10,606,000
Capital and largest city: Lisbon (pop 1,962,000)
Other large cities: Oporto (1,254,000)
Official language: Portuguese
Religion: Christianity (Roman Catholic 94%)
Government: Republic
Currency: Euro

ANDORRA

Area: 453sq km (175sq miles)
Highest point: Coma Pedrosa 2,946m (9,665ft)
Population: 71,000
Capital: Andorra La Vella (pop 21,000)
Official language: Catalan
Religion: Christianity (Roman Catholic 92%)
Government: Principality
Currency: Euro

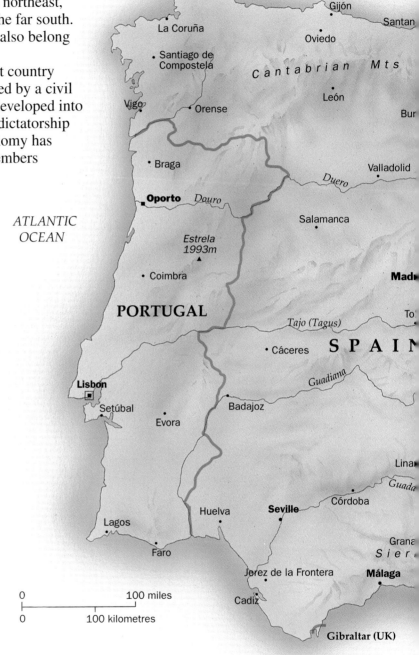

Bay of Biscay

Gijón

Santan

La Coruña

Oviedo

Santiago de Compostelá

Cantabrian Mts

León

Vigo

Orense

Bur

Braga

Valladolid

Duero

Oporto *Douro*

ATLANTIC OCEAN

Salamanca

Estrela 1993m ▲

Coimbra

Mad

PORTUGAL

Tajo (Tagus)

To

Cáceres **S P A I N**

Guadiana

Lisbon ☐

Setúbal

Badajoz

Evora

Lina

Guada

Córdoba

Huelva **Seville**

Lagos

Grana

Sier

Faro

Jerez de la Frontera **Málaga**

Cadiz

Gibraltar (UK)

| 0 | | 100 miles |
| 0 | | 100 kilometres |

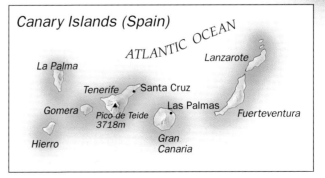

Canary Islands (Spain)

ATLANTIC OCEAN

La Palma

Lanzarote

Tenerife • Santa Cruz

Gomera

Pico de Teide 3718m

Las Palmas

Fuerteventura

Hierro

Gran Canaria

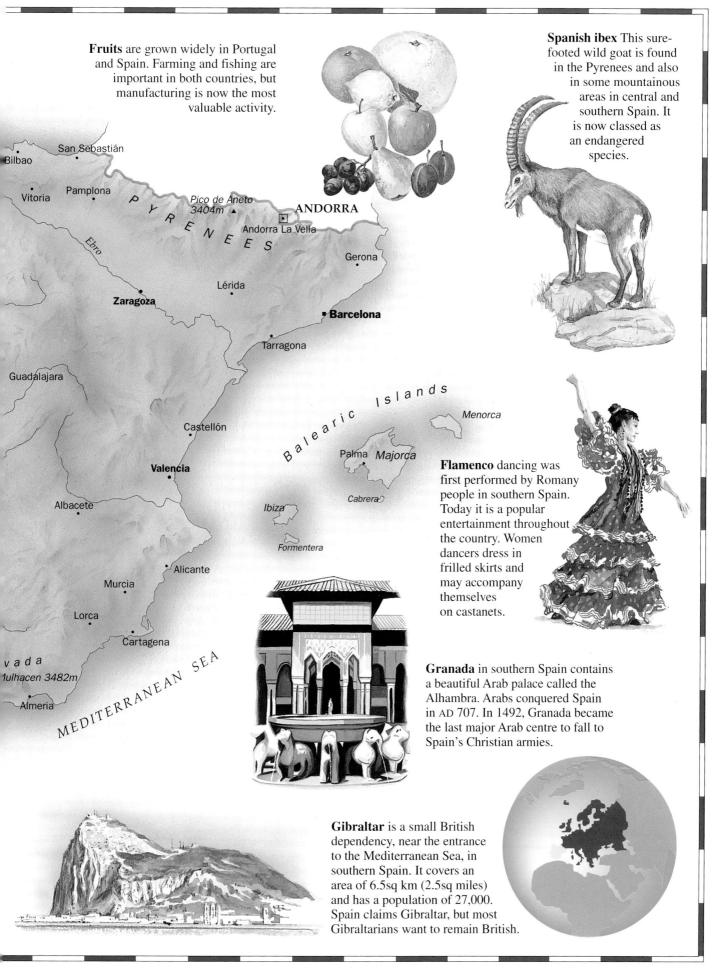

Fruits are grown widely in Portugal and Spain. Farming and fishing are important in both countries, but manufacturing is now the most valuable activity.

Spanish ibex This sure-footed wild goat is found in the Pyrenees and also in some mountainous areas in central and southern Spain. It is now classed as an endangered species.

Bilbao
San Sebastián
Vitoria
Pamplona
P Y R E N E E S
Pico de Aneto 3404m ▲
ANDORRA
Andorra La Vella
Gerona
Lérida
Ebro
Zaragoza
Barcelona
Tarragona
Guadalajara
Castellón
Balearic Islands
Menorca
Palma *Majorca*
Valencia
Cabrera
Albacete
Ibiza
Formentera
Alicante
Murcia
Lorca
Cartagena
v a d a
Mulhacen 3482m
Almeria
MEDITERRANEAN SEA

Flamenco dancing was first performed by Romany people in southern Spain. Today it is a popular entertainment throughout the country. Women dancers dress in frilled skirts and may accompany themselves on castanets.

Granada in southern Spain contains a beautiful Arab palace called the Alhambra. Arabs conquered Spain in AD 707. In 1492, Granada became the last major Arab centre to fall to Spain's Christian armies.

Gibraltar is a small British dependency, near the entrance to the Mediterranean Sea, in southern Spain. It covers an area of 6.5sq km (2.5sq miles) and has a population of 27,000. Spain claims Gibraltar, but most Gibraltarians want to remain British.

ITALY

Italy extends like a leg and foot into the Mediterranean Sea. The Alps in the far north overlook the fertile River Po basin, where most of Italy's major industrial cities are situated. The 'leg' of Italy contains the Apennine Mountains and, in the southwest, are some active volcanoes, including Etna on the island of Sicily.

Two tiny independent nations lie inside Italy. They are San Marino and Vatican City, which covers an area about the size of a town park in the city of Rome. South of Sicily is the island nation of Malta.

 ITALY

Area: 301,268sq km (116,320sq miles)
Highest point: Mont Blanc 4,807m (15,771ft)
Population: 58,134,000
Capital: Rome (pop 2,665,000)
Other large cities: Milan (4,183,000)
Naples (2,995,000)
Turin (1,247,000)
Official language: Italian
Religion: Christianity (Roman Catholic 90%)
Government: Republic
Currency: Euro

 MALTA

Area: 316sq km (122sq miles)
Population: 400,000
Capital: Valletta (pop 83,000)
Official languages: Maltese, English
Religion: Christianity (Roman Catholic 98%)
Government: Republic
Currency: Maltese lira

 SAN MARINO

Area: 61sq km (24sq miles)
Population: 29,000
Capital: San Marino (pop 4,500)
Official language: Italian
Religion: Christianity (Roman Catholic 90%)
Government: Republic
Currency: Euro

 VATICAN CITY

Area: 0.44sq km (0.17sq miles)
Population: 900
Government: Papacy
Currency: Euro

Rome The Colosseum, a huge amphitheatre dedicated in AD 79, is one of many famous ruins of the Roman Empire. Roman citizens gathered there to watch state-run spectacles, including fights between gladiators and wild animals.

Swiss Guard This body of Swiss soldiers is employed to guard the Pope. Vatican City is the headquarters of the Roman Catholic Church and the Pope is its absolute ruler.

Malta consists of several islands south of Sicily. Valletta, on the largest island, which is also called Malta, is the capital and chief port. Malta became independent from Britain in 1964, though Britain had a naval base there until 1979.

Venice is a city built on about 120 islands in the Adriatic Sea. Its streets are canals lined with beautiful buildings that are increasingly threatened by flooding, pollution and overcrowding by tourists. Italy's cities, historic sites and beautiful beaches attract about 40 million tourists to the country each year.

Style Elegant fashions and stylish cars are products that have given Italy its worldwide reputation for excellence in design. Around 50 years ago, Italy was mainly a farming country, but it has grown increasingly rich through manufacturing.

Garibaldi (1807-82) Giuseppe Garibaldi was a military hero who fought to unite Italy. In 1860, with the help of 1,000 volunteers known, as *red shirts*, he conquered Sicily.

Pompeii is an ancient Roman town near Naples. In AD 79 it was buried by volcanic ash that erupted from nearby Mount Vesuvius. The volcano has erupted many times since, the last time in 1944.

Bolzano
Trento
Udine
Treviso
erona
Venice
Trieste
Padova
Jena
Bologna
Ravenna
San Marino
SAN MARINO
Rimini
rence
Arno
Ancona
Perugia
Assisi
Tiber
Pescara
Adriatic Sea
Rome
VATICAN CITY
ITALY
Foggia
Bari
Naples
Vesuvius
Pompeii
Salerno
Potenza
Brindisi
Taranto
Tyrrhenian Sea
Catanzaro
Ustica
Lipari Is
Palermo
Messina
Trapani
Reggio di Calabria
Sicily
Etna 3340m
Catania
Licata
Pantelleria
MALTA
Valletta

0   100 miles
0   100 kilometres

23

GREECE AND THE BALKANS

This region in southeastern Europe includes Greece, the centre of a great ancient civilization, Albania, and six countries which, until the early 1990s, made up the Communist country of Yugoslavia. Following the break-up of Yugoslavia, civil wars in Bosnia and Herzegovina, Croatia and in the Kosovo region of Serbia caused great damage and loss of life. The region's land is mostly rugged. Farming is important, but manufacturing is the most valuable activity.

GREECE

Area: 131,957sq km (50,949sq miles)
Population: 10,688,000
Capital: Athens (pop 3,215,000)
Official language: Greek
Religion: Christianity (Greek Orthodox 98%)
Government: Republic
Currency: Euro

SLOVENIA

Area: 20,256sq km (7,821sq miles)
Population: 2,010,000
Capital: Ljubljana (pop 256,000)
Official language: Slovene
Religion: Christianity (Roman Catholic 58%)
Government: Republic
Currency: Tolar

CROATIA

Area: 88,117sq km (34,022sq miles)
Population: 4,495,000
Capital: Zagreb (pop 688,000)
Official language: Croatian (Serbo-Croatian)
Religion: Christianity (Roman Catholic 87%)
Government: Republic
Currency: Kuna

BOSNIA AND HERZEGOVINA

Area: 51,129sq km (19,741sq miles)
Population: 4,499,000
Capital: Sarajevo (pop 579,000)
Official language: Bosnian (Serbo-Croatian)
Religions: Christianity 46%, Islam 40%
Currency: Marka

MONTENEGRO

Area: 13,812sq km (5,333sq miles)
Population: 631,000
Capital: Podgorica (pop 152,000)
Official language: Montenegrin (Serbian)
Religions: Orthodox 69%, Islam 19%
Currency: Euro

ALBANIA

Area: 28,748sq km (11,100sq miles)
Population: 3,582,000
Capital: Tirana (pop 367,000)
Official language: Albanian
Religions: Islam, Christianity
Government: Republic
Currency: Lek

MACEDONIA

Area: 25,713sq km (9,928sq miles)
Population: 2,051,000
Capital: Skopje (pop 447,000)
Official language: Macedonian
Religions: Serbian (Macedonian) Orthodox 64%, Islam 33%
Government: Republic
Currency: Denar

SERBIA

Area: 88,361sq km (34,116sq miles)
Population: 9,396,000
Capital: Belgrade (pop 1,118,000)
Official language: Serbian (Serbo-Croatian)
Religions: Serbian Orthodox 65%, Islam 19%
Government: Republic
Currency: New dinar

Danube The middle course of this important river forms part of the boundary of Croatia. It then flows across northern Serbia. Belgrade stands at the point where the river joins the Sava, one of its main tributaries.

Marshal Tito (1892-1980) After World War II, Tito (real name, Josip Broz) served as president of Communist Yugoslavia. He kept the country united. After his death, conflict began between various language and religious groups, which led to a violent break-up of the country.

Ancient Greece was the birthplace of Western civilization. It produced great art and architecture, and influential ideas in government, philosophy and education. Pottery vases like this one are examples of many beautiful works of art that have survived since ancient times.

Goats are destructive animals. Herds of them browse on trees and graze the land until they are bare. In southeastern Europe, rain has removed the soil from bare land causing serious soil erosion.

0   100 miles
0   100 kilometres

tica

Becej

ovi Sad

Danube

Belgrade

SERBIA

Kraljevo

Morava

Nis

Kosovo

Péc

Pristina

oder

Skopje

MACEDONIA

Vardar

Tirana

Bitola

BANIA

Kavalla

Alexandroúpolis

Thessaloníka

Thasos

Véroia

▲ Mt Olympus 2917m

Limnos

Lárisa

Kérkira

fu

Vólos

Aegean Sea

Lesbos

Pindus Mts

Levkás

Khalkis

Euboea

Khios

Cephalonia

Pátrai

Andros

Samos

Athens

Piraeus

Tinos

Zákinthos

GREECE

Naxos

Kalámai

Kos

Rhodes

Rhodes

MEDITERRANEAN SEA

Khaniá

Iráklion

Crete

Dubrovnik is a beautiful medieval port and resort on the southern coast of Croatia. It was badly shelled during conflict between Croatian and Serbian forces in the 1990s.

Farming is the main activity in Albania. Crops include fruits, maize, olives, sugar beet and wheat. Albania has some mines and factories, but it remains the poorest country in Europe.

EAST-CENTRAL EUROPE

East-central Europe includes Poland, which faces the Baltic Sea. It also includes the landlocked Czech Republic and Slovakia, which until December 31, 1992, formed a single country, Czechoslovakia.

These countries had Communist governments from 1948 until the early 1990s when Communist policies were abandoned. In the 1990s, they faced many problems as they restored the land and government-owned industries to private ownership. All three nations became members of the European Union in 2004.

POLAND

Area: 323,250sq km (124,808sq miles)
Highest point: Rysy Peak 2,499m (8,199ft)
Population: 38,537,000
Capital: Warsaw (pop 2,200,000)
Other large cities: Katowice (3,069,000)
Lódz (974,000)
Kraków (859,000)
Official language: Polish
Religion: Christianity (Roman Catholic 90%)
Government: Republic
Currency: Zloty

CZECH REPUBLIC

Area: 78,864sq km (30,450sq miles)
Highest point: Snezka, in the Sudeten Mountains, 1,602m (5,256ft)
Population: 10,235,000
Capital and largest city: Prague (pop 1,170,000)
Other large cities: Brno (371,000)
Ostrava (314,000)
Official language: Czech
Religion: Christianity (Roman Catholic 26%)
Government: Republic
Currency: Czech koruna

SLOVAKIA

Area: 49,012sq km (18,924sq miles)
Highest point: Gerlachovsky Stit 2,655m (8,711ft)
Population: 5,439,000
Capital and largest city: Bratislava (pop 425,000)
Other large cities: Kosice (236,000)
Presov (93,000)
Official language: Slovak
Religion: Christianity (Roman Catholic 69%)
Government: Republic
Currency: Slovak koruna

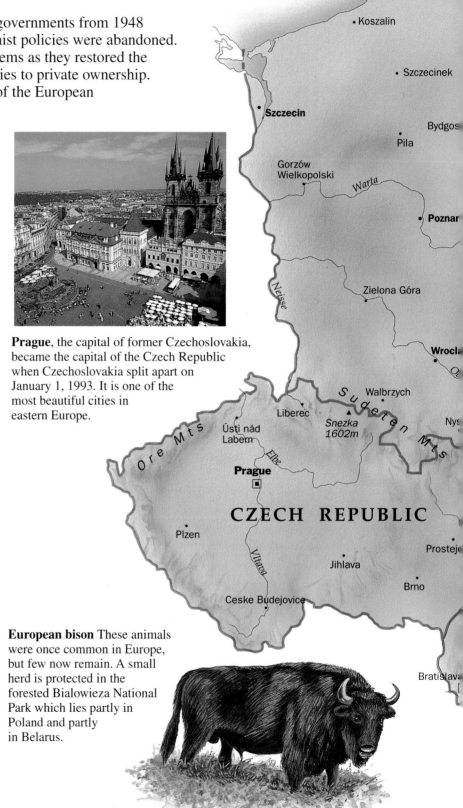

Prague, the capital of former Czechoslovakia, became the capital of the Czech Republic when Czechoslovakia split apart on January 1, 1993. It is one of the most beautiful cities in eastern Europe.

European bison These animals were once common in Europe, but few now remain. A small herd is protected in the forested Bialowieza National Park which lies partly in Poland and partly in Belarus.

0 | 100 miles
0 | 100 kilometres

ynia

·Elblag

·ansk

Elk

·Olsztyn

Bialystok

·Torun

Wloclawek

Bug

Warsaw

L A N D

·**Lódź**

Radom

·Lublin

Kielce

Czestochowa

Vistula

Katowice

Rzeszów

Gliwice

Kraków

Przemysl

ava

Bielsko-Biala

)strava

C a r p a t h i a n   M t s

Rysy Peak 2499m

Gerlachovsky Stit 2655m

·Presov

·Poprad

Kosice

SLOVAKIA

·Zvolen

·Nitra

Pope John Paul II was born in Poland. He became Pope in 1978 and died in 2005. The Communists discouraged religious worship, but many Poles kept their faith in Christianity and opposed Communist rule in their country.

Industry developed rapidly in Poland and other parts of eastern Europe under Communist rule. Factories powered by coal and oil have caused severe pollution over large areas.

Bratislava is the capital of Slovakia, which was created on January 1, 1993. Bratislava stands on the River Danube. Its factories make chemicals, machinery, petroleum products and textiles.

SOUTHEASTERN EUROPE

Southeastern Europe contains landlocked Hungary and two countries, Romania and Bulgaria, which have coastlines on the Black Sea. All three countries had mainly agricultural economies until they came under Communist rule in the late 1940s. Today manufacturing is the most valuable activity. In the 1990s, the countries overcame problems as they worked to restore democracy and private ownership of all economic activity. Hungary joined the European Union in 2004, and the other two countries in 2007.

HUNGARY

Area: 93,032sq km (35,920sq miles)
Highest point: Mount Kekes 1,015m (3,330ft)
Population: 9,981,000
Capital and largest city: Budapest (pop 1,708,000)
Other large cities: Debrecen (206,000)
Miskolc (180,000)
Official language: Hungarian
Religion: Christianity (Roman Catholic 51%, Protestant 20%)
Government: Republic
Currency: Forint

ROMANIA

Area: 238,391sq km (92,043sq miles)
Highest point: Mount Moldoveanu 2,543m (8,343ft)
Population: 22,304,000
Capital and largest city: Bucharest (pop 1,853,000)
Other large cities: Constanta (310,000)
Iasi (340,000)
Official language: Romanian
Religion: Christianity (Eastern Orthodox 90%)
Government: Republic
Currency: New Leu

BULGARIA

Area: 110,912sq km (42,823sq miles)
Highest point: Musala Peak 2,925m (9,596ft)
Population: 7,385,000
Capital and largest city: Sofia (pop 1,076,000)
Other large cities: Plovdiv (338,000)
Varna (321,000)
Official language: Bulgarian
Religions: Christianity (Bulgarian Orthodox 84%), Islam 12%
Government: Republic
Currency: Lev

Wheat is the leading grain crop in southeastern Europe. Maize is also important. Other food crops include fruits, potatoes, sugar beet and various vegetables.

Budapest, the capital of Hungary, stands on the River Danube. Tourists visit the city to see its many historic buildings, but Budapest also has many factories, producing such things as chemical products, textiles and transport equipment.

Wild boars were once common in the forests of central Europe. But most of the original forests have been cut down to make way for farms and cities. Wild boars, along with many other plant and animal species, are now rare.

0 — 100 miles
0 — 100 kilometres

Dracula, a fictional character, was a vampire who was supposed to have lived in Transylvania, Romania. Legends of vampires may have started because of the many brutal murders committed in the 15th century by Vlad Tepes, a prince who ruled in the region.

Tobacco is grown in southeastern Europe, where it flourishes during the warm and sunny summers. Winters are cold but only severe when icy winds blow from the north.

Wine is produced in all three countries in southeastern Europe, and Romania and Hungary rank among the world's top twenty producers. Many of the wines of this region are exported to western Europe.

Roses are grown in Bulgaria to make attar of roses. Only the petals of red roses are used to produce this fragrant oil, which is an ingredient of expensive perfumes. A less fragrant attar is made from a white rose.

Satu Mare
Baja Mare
Dej
Cluj-Napoca
Tîrgu Mures
Botosani
Iasi
Piatra-Neamt
Bacau

ROMANIA

Carpathian Mts
Prut
Siret

Mures
Hunedoara
Sibiu
Moldoveanu 2543m
Brasov
Transylvanian Alps
Galati
Mouths of the Danube
Buzau
Braila
Ploiesti
Pitesti
Craiova
Olt
■ **Bucharest**
Danube
Constanta
din
Ruse
Dobrich
Mikhaylovgrad
Pleven
Veliko Târnovo
Varna
Balkan Mts
BULGARIA
BLACK SEA
Burgas
■ **Sofia**
Stara Zagora
Musala Peak 2925m
Plovdiv
Blagoevgrad

29

EASTERN EUROPE

When the Soviet Union broke up in December 1991, following the collapse of Communism, the 15 republics that made up the Soviet Union became independent nations. The map of eastern Europe shown here contains six of them. In the 1990s, the governments of the new countries worked to set up new democratic political, legal and economic systems. Three of these new democratic countries, Estonia, Latvia and Lithuania, became members of the European Union in 2004.

ESTONIA

Area: 45,100sq km (17,413sq miles)
Population: 1,324,000
Capital: Tallinn (pop 391,000)
Official language: Estonian
Religion: Christianity (28%)
Government: Republic
Currency: Kroon

LATVIA

Area: 64,600sq km (24,924sq miles)
Population: 2,275,000
Capital: Riga (pop 733,000)
Official language: Latvian
Religion: Christianity (40%)
Government: Republic
Currency: Lat

LITHUANIA

Area: 65,200sq km (25,174sq miles)
Population: 3,586,000
Capital: Vilnius (pop 549,000)
Official language: Lithuanian
Religion: Christianity (Roman Catholic 79%)
Government: Republic
Currency: Litas

BELARUS

Area: 207,600sq km (80,155sq miles)
Population: 10,293,000
Capital: Minsk (pop 1,705,000)
Official languages: Belarussian, Russian
Religion: Christianity (Eastern Othodox 80%)
Government: Republic
Currency: Belarussian rouble

UKRAINE

Area: 603,700sq km (233,090sq miles)
Population: 46,711,000
Capital: Kiev (pop 2,618,000)
Official language: Ukrainian
Religion: Christianity (43%)
Government: Republic
Currency: Hryvnia

MOLDOVA

Area: 33,700sq km (13,012sq miles)
Population: 4,467,000
Capital: Chisinau (pop 662,000)
Official language: Romanian
Religion: Christianity (Eastern Orthodox 98%)
Government: Republic
Currency: Moldovan leu

Ukraine has been called the breadbasket of Europe because of the amount of wheat it grows on its vast plains. It also ranks as one of the world's top producers of sugar beet. Wheat is grown throughout eastern Europe.

Amber is the hardened resin of ancient pine trees that grew in northern Europe millions of years ago. A large amount is found along the Baltic Sea coasts of Estonia, Latvia and Lithuania. It is used in jewellery.

100 miles

100 kilometres

Chernobyl, near Kiev in Ukraine, was the site of the worst nuclear accident in history. An explosion at its nuclear power plant in 1986 released radioactive substances into the atmosphere which were carried by winds into northern and western Europe.

Riga is the capital of Latvia. It stands on the Gulf of Riga and has beautiful medieval buildings. It is also a major industrial city, producing chemicals, electronics and machinery.

tsyebsk

Mahilyow

ruysk

Homyel

hernobyl

■ **Kiev**

U K R A I N E

■ **Kharkov**

Poltava

Kramatorsk

Luhansk

Horlivka

Dneprodzerzinsk

Dnepropetrovsk

• Makiyivka

Kryvyy Rih •

• **Zaporozje**

Donetsk

Mariupol'

Kherson

Dnepr

Melitopol

Odessa

Sea of Azov

Simferopol'

Sevastopol

Black Sea

Wolves, which are one of the ancestors of domestic dogs, are found throughout eastern Europe. They live mostly in open country where there is cover. Their numbers have been greatly reduced by hunting.

Flax is a leading crop in Belarus and Ukraine. These two countries are among the world's top ten producers. Flax fibre is used to make linen, and the seeds to make linseed oil.

EUROPEAN RUSSIA

Only part of Russia, the world's largest country, is in Europe. The rest is in Asia. Russia had a troubled history in the 20th century. In 1917, Communists took power. From 1922, Russia became the major part of the vast Soviet Union. In World War II (1939-45), German forces invaded European Russia and caused great destruction. In 1991, after Communism had failed to solve the country's problems, the Soviet Union broke up into 15 countries. The largest of these is Russia.

RUSSIA

Area: 17,075.400sq km (6,592,850sq miles), of which about 25% is in Europe
Highest point: Mount Elbrus, in the Caucasus Mountains, 5,642m (18,510ft)
Population: 142,894,000 (about 80% of whom live in European Russia)
Capital and largest city: Moscow (pop 10,469,000)
Other large cities (in European Russia):
St Petersburg (5,214,000)
Nizhniy Novgorod (1,331,000)
Samara (1,260,000)
Kazan (1,100,000)
Official language: Russian
Religions: Christianity (Russian Orthodox 16%), Islam 10%
Government: Republic
Currency: Rouble

ASIAN RUSSIA
Asian Russia is thinly populated. Though three-quarters of Russia is in Asia, it contains only 20 per cent of Russia's people.

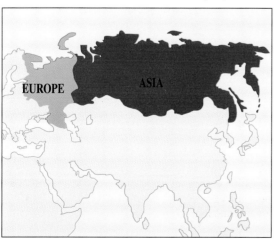

Hammer and sickle
This Communist symbol appeared in yellow on the red flag that was used by the former Soviet Union. It represented the nation's industrial and agricultural workers.

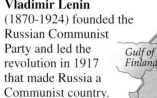

Vladimir Lenin
(1870-1924) founded the Russian Communist Party and led the revolution in 1917 that made Russia a Communist country.

Icons are religious paintings found in Eastern Orthodox churches. The Communists discouraged religious worship, but Christianity survived. The Russian Orthodox Church is the largest religious denomination in Russia.

Murmans

Lake Onega

Lake Ladoga

Gulf of Finland

St Petersburg

Cherepov

Novgorod

Moscov

Kaluga .

Tu

Smolensk

0   200 miles
0   200 kilometres

Sea of Azov

Bla c

Ballet is one of Russia's major art forms. The Kirov Ballet of St Petersburg and the Bolshoi Theatre Ballet in Moscow are world famous. Russian composers include Nikolai Rimsky-Korsakov, Peter Ilich Tchaikovsky and Igor Stravinsky.

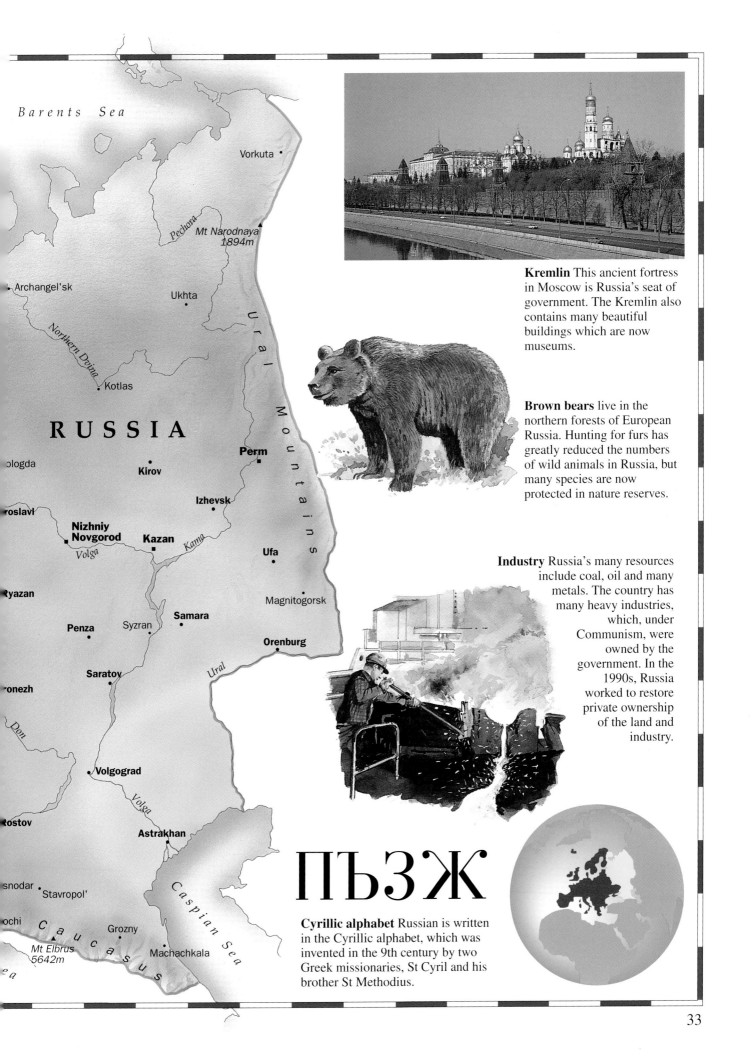

Barents Sea

Vorkuta •

Pechora
Mt Narodnaya
1894m

• Archangel'sk

Ukhta •

Northern Dvina

• Kotlas

R U S S I A

Ural Mountains

ologda

Kirov

Perm

Izhevsk

roslavl

Nizhniy Novgorod   **Kazan**

Volga   *Kama*

Ufa

Ryazan

Magnitogorsk

Penza   Syzran   **Samara**

Orenburg

onezh

Saratov   *Ural*

• **Don**

Volgograd

Volga

Rostov

Astrakhan

Caspian Sea

snodar

Stavropol'

ochi

Caucasus

Grozny

Mt Elbrus
5642m

Machachkala

a

Kremlin This ancient fortress in Moscow is Russia's seat of government. The Kremlin also contains many beautiful buildings which are now museums.

Brown bears live in the northern forests of European Russia. Hunting for furs has greatly reduced the numbers of wild animals in Russia, but many species are now protected in nature reserves.

Industry Russia's many resources include coal, oil and many metals. The country has many heavy industries, which, under Communism, were owned by the government. In the 1990s, Russia worked to restore private ownership of the land and industry.

ПЪЗЖ

Cyrillic alphabet Russian is written in the Cyrillic alphabet, which was invented in the 9th century by two Greek missionaries, St Cyril and his brother St Methodius.

People and Beliefs

Europe is the home of about 11 per cent of the world's population. It ranks third among the continents in population, after Asia and Africa, which overtook it in the late 1990s. Large parts of northern Europe contain few people, but the central plains of Europe and the Mediterranean region contain some of the most densely populated areas in the world. Many people live in huge cities. Europe's largest cities include Paris, Moscow, London, Berlin and Athens.

Population densities in Europe
Number of people per square kilometre

- Over 100
- Between 50 and 100
- Between 10 and 50
- Between 1 and 10
- Below 1

- ■ Cities of more than 1,000,000 people
- • Cities of more than 500,000 people

Population and area

Although only 25 per cent of Russia lies in Europe, it is by far the largest country in Europe both in area and in population. Ukraine, another country created in 1991 when the Soviet Union broke up, is the second largest country, although in population it ranks sixth.

Germany has the second largest population in Europe, although it ranks only sixth in area. The third most populous European country is the much smaller United Kingdom, which ranks eleventh in area.

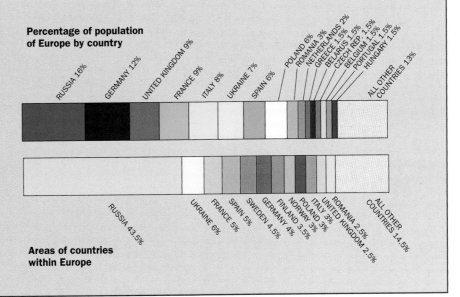

Percentage of population of Europe by country

RUSSIA 16% · GERMANY 12% · UNITED KINGDOM 9% · FRANCE 9% · ITALY 8% · UKRAINE 7% · SPAIN 6% · POLAND 6% · ROMANIA 3% · NETHERLANDS 2% · GREECE 1.5% · BELARUS 1.5% · CZECH REP. 1.5% · BELGIUM 1.5% · PORTUGAL 1.5% · HUNGARY 1.5% · ALL OTHER COUNTRIES 13%

Areas of countries within Europe

RUSSIA 43.5% · UKRAINE 6% · FRANCE 5% · SPAIN 5% · SWEDEN 4.5% · GERMANY 4% · FINLAND 3.5% · NORWAY 3% · POLAND 3% · ITALY 3% · UNITED KINGDOM 2.5% · ROMANIA 2.5% · ALL OTHER COUNTRIES 14.5%

Main religious groups

Christianity, the main religion in Europe, has played an important part in the continent's history, and the great Christian cathedrals testify to its influence on art and architecture.

Roman Catholics make up the largest single group. With their headquarters in Rome, they are strongest in southern Europe and parts of eastern Europe, especially Poland. The other main groups are the Orthodox and the Protestants. Orthodox Christians live chiefly in Greece, the southern nations in eastern Europe and Russia. Protestants live in the northern countries of western Europe. Europe also has Jewish and Islamic communities. Jews live in most parts of Europe, while Muslims live in the Balkans and also in countries, such as France and Germany, which have large numbers of immigrants from North Africa and Southeast Asia.

Under Communism, religious worship was discouraged, but today everyone has freedom of worship. Many people in eastern Europe and elsewhere in Europe do not follow any religion.

Legend:
- Roman Catholic
- Orthodox
- Orthodox and Islamic
- Protestant
- Protestant and Roman Catholic

The great medieval cathedrals of Europe are architectural masterpieces that contain priceless works of art. Thousands of people visit them every year.

CLIMATE AND VEGETATION

Europe's climates range from polar and tundra in the northeast to Mediterranean in the south. The northwest has a mild climate, because temperatures are raised by a warm offshore current, called the North Atlantic Drift – the northern part of the Gulf Stream, which starts in the Gulf of Mexico. Northern Europe has large cold forests of coniferous trees. The natural vegetation of most of central Europe was deciduous forest, with trees that shed their leaves in autumn. Most of this deciduous forest has been cut down to create farmland and space for cities.

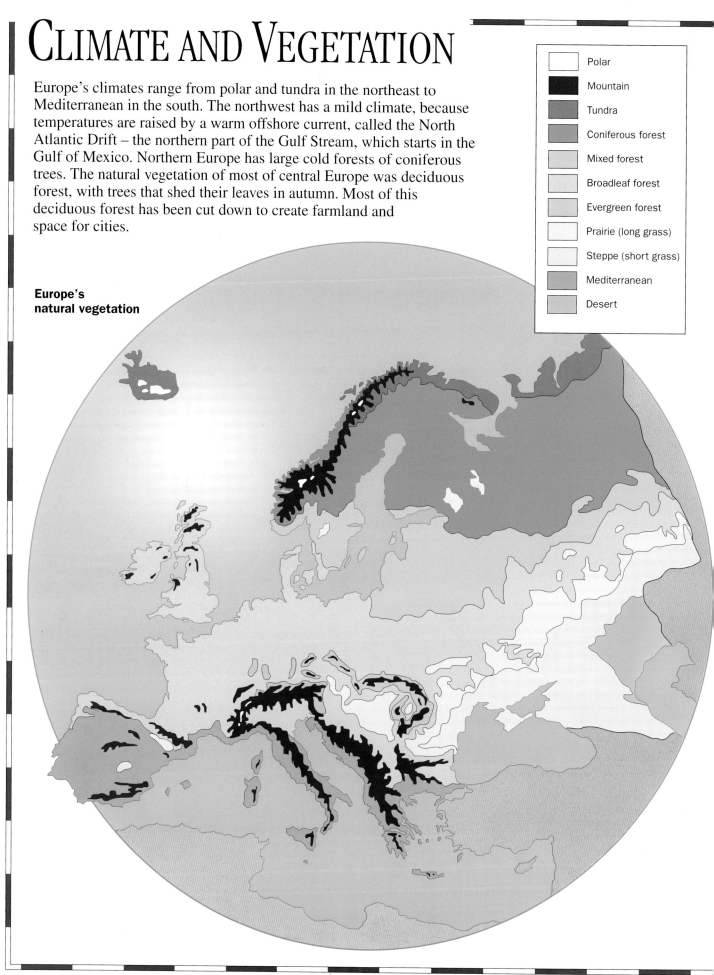

Europe's natural vegetation

	Polar
	Mountain
	Tundra
	Coniferous forest
	Mixed forest
	Broadleaf forest
	Evergreen forest
	Prairie (long grass)
	Steppe (short grass)
	Mediterranean
	Desert

Summer temperatures

Winter temperatures

Temperature
key scale in °C

-24 to -16	0 to 8
-16 to -8	8 to 16
-8 to 0	16 to 24
	24 to 32

Range of climates

Europe's climate varies from the cold north to the warm temperate south. The climate also changes from west to east. In the west, the climate is influenced by the Atlantic Ocean. The ocean makes summers milder and winters warmer. To the east, the climate becomes more extreme, with hotter summers and bitterly cold winters. Rainfall in eastern Europe is generally less than in the west.

Ranges of vegetation

The three main types of vegetation in Europe are treeless tundra, forests and grasslands. (Mountains, which get colder with altitude, also have these three types of vegetation.) In the coldest northern regions, summers are short. When the topsoil thaws, low plants grow, providing food for herds of reindeer and other animals. The northern forests contain conifer trees that can survive the cold winters. Farther south are mixed forests of evergreen and deciduous trees. Central and southern Europe have broadleaf forests, containing ash, birch, beech, maple and oak. In the Mediterranean, many trees, including pines, cork oaks and olives, have tough leaves that retain moisture during the hot summers and stay on the trees all year. Grasslands occur in regions with dry climates. The best-known grasslands are in Ukraine and southern European Russia. They are called the steppes.

Annual rainfall
in mm

	Above 1500
	1000 - 1500
	750 - 1000
	500 - 750
	0 - 500

ECOLOGY AND ENVIRONMENT

Europe is a prosperous continent, but economic development has caused great damage to the environment. Farming has destroyed natural habitats, harming wildlife. Industry has also caused pollution – in the air, rivers and seas, and also on land – and contributed to global warming. Pollution from one country often spreads to others. Today, the governments of most European countries are working to prevent further damage.

Seals have suffered greatly in recent years from oil spills and the dumping of toxic wastes.

ICELAND

NORWAY

FINLAND

SWEDEN

ESTONIA

LATVIA

DENMARK

LITHUANIA

KALININGRAD (RUSSIA)

RUSSIA

BELARUS

Oil spills

IRELAND

UNITED KINGDOM

Oil spills

Flood

NETHERLANDS

Flood

POLAND

Oil spills

BELGIUM

GERMANY

LUXEMBOURG

CZECH REP.

Nuclear accident

SLOVAKIA

UKRAINE

Oil spills

FRANCE

SWITZERLAND

AUSTRIA

HUNGARY

MOLDOVA

ROMANIA

SLOVENIA

Flood

CROATIA

Flood

SPAIN

ANDORRA

BOSNIA& HERZEGOVINA

SERBIA

PORTUGAL

ITALY

MONTENEGRO

BULGARIA

MACEDONIA

Earthquake

ALBANIA

GREECE

Earthquake

MALTA

Environmental damage to land and sea

- ▢ Area affected by acid rain
- ▢ Area at risk of desertification
- ▢ Most polluted seas
- ─ Most polluted rivers
- ▼ Sea dumping sites
- ● Worst urban polluters
- ● Major environmental disasters and type

Natural hazards

Volcanic eruptions occur in southern Italy and Iceland, while earthquakes affect some areas, especially the eastern Mediterranean. Global warming caused by air pollution has begun to change weather patterns.

Unusual weather, such as exceptionally heavy rains and storms, has caused severe floods in some areas, such as France and UK, while extremely high summer temperatures have caused thousands of deaths.

Damaging the environment

The use of smokeless fuels has greatly reduced air pollution in many European cities, but factories, power stations and motor vehicles still pump poisonous gases into the air. These gases are dissolved by water droplets in the air and return to the ground as acid rain. The chemicals kill trees and wildlife in rivers and lakes. Air pollution has also caused global warming and damage to the ozone layer, which protects us from the sun's harmful ultraviolet radiation.

Intensive farming in dry areas, such as southeastern Spain, has turned once fertile land into barren desert. Industrial and agricultural wastes have polluted rivers, while oil spills from tankers have greatly harmed marine life.

Accidents at nuclear power stations have released dangerous nuclear fallout. Europe's worst nuclear accident occurred when explosions and fire damaged a nuclear power plant at Chernobyl, Ukraine, in 1986.

Diseases and deaths

The leading causes of death in western Europe are circulatory diseases (which cause heart attacks and strokes), cancers and car accidents.

Number of deaths each year from cancer per 100,000 people

| 200 | 225 | 250 | 275 | 300 + |

Number of deaths each year from heart disease per 100,000 people

| 100 | 150 | 200 | 250 | 300 + |

Number of deaths each year from road traffic accidents per 100,000 people

| 10 | 15 | 20 | 25 | 30 + |

Eastern European figures not available

Endangered species

During the Ice Age, a lot of animals became extinct as the ice sheets advanced and retreated. However, since the end of the Ice Age, about 10,000 years ago, the land has been transformed into a patchwork of farms and towns. The destruction of habitats has led to some extinctions, while many animals have disappeared from areas that they once inhabited.

Hunting for food and skins, and the slaughter of animals such as bears and wolves to protect domestic animals, have also reduced the ranges of many creatures. Pressures on wildlife remain as the continuing destruction of hedgerows, land reclamation, military exercises and the growth of tourism continue to reduce natural habitats.

Ladies-slipper orchid

Some endangered species in Europe

Mammals
European bison
Horseshoe bat
Ibex
Lynx
Otter

Birds and butterflies
Dalmatian pelican
Golden eagle
Swallowtail butterfly

Marine animals
Common seal
Loggerhead turtle

Trees and plants
Bog pimpernel
Dwarf birch
Irish spurge
Ladies-slipper orchid

ECONOMY

Most European countries are highly developed. They produce large amounts of manufactured goods and farm products, but have to import food and many raw materials. Until the late 1980s, the economies of the Communist countries of eastern Europe were run by their governments but today virtually all of them encourage private ownership and free enterprise.

European Union
To increase trade and to encourage economic growth 27 countries (see right) belong to the European Union, and several others, including Croatia, Macedonia and Turkey, hope to join soon. Some 13 of the nations now share a currency, the euro €.

€ Austria
€ Belgium
Bulgaria
Cyprus*
Czech Republic
Denmark
Estonia
€ Finland
€ France
€ Germany
€ Greece
Hungary
€ Ireland
€ Italy

Latvia
Lithuania
€ Luxembourg
€ Malta
Poland
€ Portugal
Romania
Slovakia
Slovenia
€ Spain
Sweden
€ Netherlands
United Kingdom

The wealth of Europe comes from

- ✈ Aviation
- 🐐 Cotton
- 🐟 Fishing
- 🌲 Forest products
- 🍎 Fruits
- 🍃 Gas
- 💻 High-tech industries
- 🐄 Livestock
- 🏭 Manufacturing
- ⚒ Mining and minerals
- 🛢 Oil
- 🫒 Olive oil
- 🐑 Sheep/wool
- 🌱 Tobacco
- ⚒ Tourism
- 🌾 Wheat
- 🍇 Wines

*Though geographically in Asia, Cyprus is in the EU. For more information about Cyprus, see Continents in Close-up Asia

Gross domestic product

In order to compare the economies of countries, experts work out the gross domestic product (GDP) of the countries in United States dollars. The GDP is the total value of the goods and services produced by a country in a year. The chart, right, shows that the countries with the highest GDPs in 2005 were Germany, the United Kingdom, France, and Italy. The combined GDP of the 27 members of the European Union is one-tenth larger than that of the United States.

GDP for the countries of Europe (in billions of dollars)

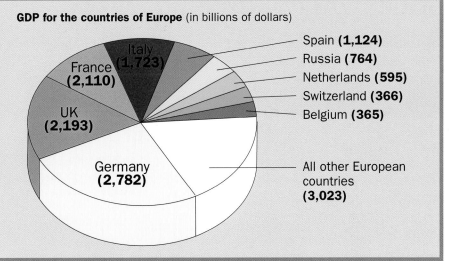

- Italy (1,723)
- France (2,110)
- UK (2,193)
- Germany (2,782)
- Spain (1,124)
- Russia (764)
- Netherlands (595)
- Switzerland (366)
- Belgium (365)
- All other European countries (3,023)

Sources of energy

Coal and hydroelectricity were once the chief sources of power in Europe. Major coal producers are Russia, Ukraine and Poland. Hydroelectricity is important in rainy mountainous countries, such as Norway.

Today, oil and natural gas have become major sources of power, while coal has become less important. Europe's oil producers include Britain and Norway, which share the oilfields in the North Sea, and Russia. Leading natural gas producers include Britain, the Netherlands, Norway and Russia. Major nuclear power-producing countries include France, Germany and Russia. Other sources of energy, including tidal, wind and wave power, are now being developed in Europe.

Per capita GDPs

Per capita means per head or per person. Per capita GDPs are worked out by dividing the GDP by the population. For example, the per capita GDP of the oil-rich country of Norway is US $42,800. By contrast, Albania has a per capita GDP of only $5,300, which places it among the world's poorest countries.

Sources of energy found in Europe

- 🛢 Oil
- 🪔 Gas
- ≈ Hydroelectricity
- ⚒ Coal
- ☢ Uranium

POLITICS AND HISTORY

Between the late 1940s and the 1980s, the democratic countries of the West were opposed to the Communist countries in the east. The tension between the groups was called the Cold War. In the 1980s, the collapse of Communism in the Soviet Union and eastern Europe led to the appearance of new countries on the map. In the 1990s, the West helped the former Communist countries to rebuild their economies. The Cold War was over but new kinds of conflict began. In particular, civil wars occurred when rival language and religious groups fought for power in Chechnya, Russia, and in former Yugoslavia.

The Romans dominated Europe with their army. Foot soldiers regularly marched vast distances carrying equipment weighing more than 40kg (88lb).

Great events
After the end of the Ice Age, around 10,000 years ago, the warm climate led to a rapid growth in the human population of Europe. Around 5,000 years ago, civilizations began to develop in the eastern Mediterranean and, between 500 and 300 BC, the ancient Greek civilization reached its peak. It was succeeded by the Roman empire which developed building, law and commerce.

Following the fall of the Roman empire, there was a period of decline. The early 14th century, however, saw the beginning of a period, known for its brilliant art and a revival of learning, called the Renaissance. Towards the end of this period in the 15th and 16th centuries, Europeans began to spread around the world.

The Industrial Revolution began in Europe in the late 18th century. In the late 19th century, Europeans colonized much of the world. The 20th century saw two major world wars and frequent changes to the map of Europe. The European empires and the Cold War came to an end and the century ended with the hope that co-operation between countries could prevent conflict. However, with the new century have come new terrorist threats.

William the Conqueror defeats the Anglo-Saxons 1066

Vikings begin raiding western Europe 793

Russian Revolution 1917

Irish Potato Famine 1845

Mongols invade from the east 1236

Napoleon defeated at Waterloo 1815

Berlin Wall erected 1961

Spanish Armada defeated 1588

Gutenberg prints first book 1445

Communists take over most of eastern Europe 1948

French Revolution 1789

Reformation begins in Germany 1517

Black Death spreads through Europe from southern ports 1346

Visigoths sack Rome AD410 ending the thousand-year empire

Greek civilizations begin 3200 BC

20,000 Evidence of cave dwellers in various sites throughout Europe

6500 Farming in Greece

3200 Early Cycladic civilization in Aegean

1600 Rise of Mycenaean civilization in Greece

1200 Collapse of Mycenaean empire

509 Foundation of Roman Republic

400s Ancient Greece reaches its peak

334 Alexander the Great begins his conquests of eastern Europe, Asia and North Africa

43 Roman invasion of Britain

117 Greatest extent of the Roman empire

410 Visigoths sack Rome

711 Muslim conquest of Spain

793 Viking raids begin

1066 Norman conquest of England

1236 Mongols from Asia attack eastern Europe

1275 Italian explorer Marco Polo reaches China

1290 Spectacles invented in Italy

1337 Hundred Years War between England and France starts

1348 Black Death spreads Asia, killing an estim 20 million pec

20,000 BC

AD 1

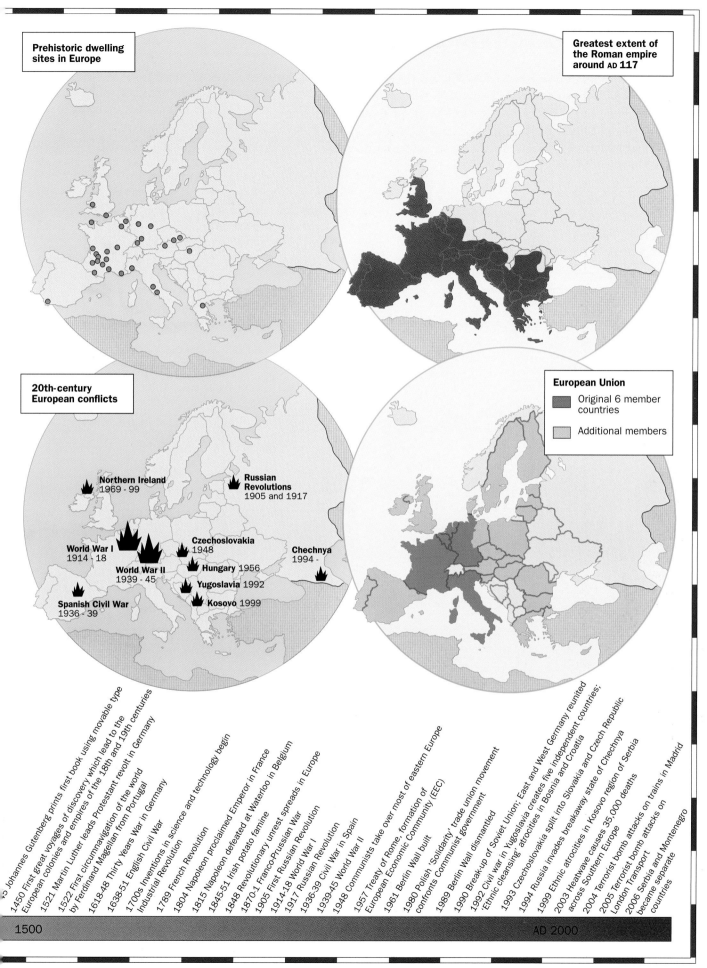

Prehistoric dwelling sites in Europe

Greatest extent of the Roman empire around AD 117

20th-century European conflicts

Northern Ireland
1969 - 99

Russian Revolutions
1905 and 1917

World War I
1914 - 18

Czechoslovakia
1948

Chechnya
1994 -

World War II
1939 - 45

Hungary 1956

Yugoslavia 1992

Spanish Civil War
1936 - 39

Kosovo 1999

European Union

Original 6 member countries

Additional members

1500

AD 2000

1450 Johannes Gutenberg prints first book using movable type
First great voyages of discovery which lead to the European colonies and empires of the 18th and 19th centuries
1521 Martin Luther leads Protestant revolt in Germany
1522 First circumnavigation of the world by Ferdinand Magellan from Portugal
1618-48 Thirty Years War in Germany
1638-51 English Civil War
1700s Inventions in science and technology begin Industrial Revolution
1789 French Revolution
1804 Napoleon proclaimed Emperor in France
1815 Napoleon defeated at Waterloo in Belgium
1845-51 Irish potato famine
1848 Revolutionary unrest spreads in Europe
1870-1 Franco-Prussian War
1905 First Russian Revolution
1914-18 World War I
1917 Russian Revolution
1936-39 Civil War in Spain
1939-45 World War II
1948 Communists take over most of eastern Europe
1957 Treaty of Rome, formation of European Economic Community (EEC)
1961 Berlin Wall built
1980 Polish 'Solidarity' trade union movement confronts Communist government
1989 Berlin Wall dismantled
1990 Break-up of Soviet Union; East and West Germany reunited
1992 Civil war in Yugoslavia creates five independent countries; 'Ethnic cleansing' atrocities in Bosnia and Croatia
1993 Czechoslovakia split into Slovakia and Czech Republic
1994 Russia invades breakaway state of Chechnya
1999 Ethnic atrocities in Kosovo region of Serbia
2003 Heatwave causes 35,000 deaths across Southern Europe
2004 Terrorist bomb attacks on trains in Madrid
2005 Terrorist bomb attacks on London Transport
2006 Serbia and Montenegro became separate countries

43

ATLANTIC OCEAN

The Atlantic is the world's second largest ocean after the Pacific. It stretches from the Arctic Ocean around the North Pole to the icy continent of Antarctica around the South Pole. Greenland is the largest of the many islands in the Atlantic Ocean.

Strong currents move through the Atlantic. The warm Gulf Stream starts in the Gulf of Mexico and flows northeast to Europe. It warms coastal areas in northwest Europe. By contrast, the icy Labrador Current flows south from the Arctic and chills the northeastern coasts of North America.

GREENLAND (Denmark)
Norwegian Sea
ICELAND
North Sea
IRELAND UK
EUROPE
NORTH AMERICA
NORTH ATLANTIC OCEAN
Azores (Portugal)
Mediterranean Sea
Bermuda (UK)
Madeira (Portugal)
Canary Is. (Spain)
Gulf of Mexico
Tropic of Cancer
Puerto Rico Trench
CAPE VERDE IS
AFRICA
Caribbean Sea
St Peter and St Paul Rocks (Brazil)
Equator
Fernando de Noronha (Brazil)
Ascension (UK)
SOUTH AMERICA
Trindade (Brazil)
St Helena (UK)
Tropic of Capricorn
SOUTH ATLANTIC OCEAN
Tristan da Cunha (UK)
Gough I. (UK)
Falkland Is. (UK)
Bouvet I. (Norway)
South Georgia (UK)

ATLANTIC OCEAN
Area: about 106,000,000sq km (41,000,000sq miles)
Average depth: 3,580m (about 11,700ft)
Deepest point: Milwaukee Deep, in the Puerto Rico Trench, 8,648m (28,374ft)

Charles Lindbergh (1902-74), an American aviator, made the first solo non-stop flight across the Atlantic Ocean in May 1927. Today the ocean is a busy highway and is extremely important in world trade.

Spirit of St. Louis

ARCTIC OCEAN

The Arctic is the smallest of the world's four oceans. It is bordered by North America, Asia and northwestern Europe. It is linked to the Atlantic by the broad Norwegian Sea. The North Pole lies near its centre.

Sea ice covers much of the Arctic Ocean, and this stopped early explorers from finding a sea passage that would be a short cut from Europe to the Far East. They searched for a northeast passage north of Asia and a northwest passage north of North America. The first voyage through the Northeast Passage around Asia took place in 1878-9 and the first through the Northwest Passage was first completed in 1906. Neither route was good for trade.

PACIFIC OCEAN

Bering Sea

60°

Arctic Circle

70°

Permanent pack ice

Beaufort Sea

NORTH AMERICA

80°

180°

Laptev Sea

ASIA

120°

120°

ARCTIC OCEAN

North Pole

Severnaya Zemlya (Russia)

Hudson Bay

Ellesmere I.

60°

60°

Kara Sea

Baffin Bay

Franz Josef Land (Russia)

Novaya Zemlya (Russia)

0°

Svalbard (Norway)

Greenland Sea

Barents Sea

GREENLAND (Denmark)

Labrador Sea

Limit of Winter pack ice

Norwegian Sea

ICELAND

ATLANTIC OCEAN

EUROPE

Robert E Peary (1856-1920), a US Navy Commander, was the first explorer to reach the North Pole. He crossed the sea ice with his assistant Matthew Henson and four Inuits, reaching the Pole on April 6, 1909.

ARCTIC OCEAN

Area: about 13,230,000sq km (5,110,000sq miles)
Average depth: 1,120m (about 3,670ft)
Deepest point: about 5,550m (18,044ft) north of Svalbard

INDEX

Numbers in **bold** are map references
Numbers in *italics* are picture references

Picture credits
Photographs: British Airways 11
EEC 4
The Hutchison Library 5, 11, 15, 19, 26, 27, 28, 31
Travel Photo International 5, 6, 12, 23, 25, 33, 35